C. Justice

SURVIVING THE ABUSE ADDICTION

Limited Special Edition. No. 22 of 25 Paperbacks

The author was born in Jamaica. At the age of nine, she moved to Winnipeg, MB. It was a cold welcome to Canada. The experience of being a Canadian-Jamaican has made an incredible impact on her life. She loves herself more every day. Through her writing, she has found a powerful outlet to free her mind.

The author has been abused, heartbroken and betrayed; she has loved and been loved. Everything she has written in this book is to inspire others that no matter what the odds, you can overcome them. Rise above it all to be strong and free.

C. Justice

SURVIVING THE ABUSE ADDICTION

AUSTIN MACAULEY PUBLISHERS™

LONDON • CAMBRIDGE • NEW YORK • SHARJAH

A CIP catalogue record for this title is available from the British Library.

ISBN 9781528938839 (Paperback)
ISBN 9781528938846 (Hardback)
ISBN 9781528969727 (ePub e-book)

www.austinmacauley.com

First Published (2020)
Austin Macauley Publishers Ltd
25 Canada Square
Canary Wharf
London
E14 5LQ

First of all, I would like to thank God for delivering me from this learning season in my life. I would also like to acknowledge and thank all my family and friends who were with me during this time, helping me to see that I was not alone.

Table of Contents

Introduction

"There's no present like the time."

A quote I heard in a movie, 'The Second Best Exotic Marigold Hotel', such a profound and simple play on words. We take time for granted, forgetting that it is in fact a present indeed. We see so many people who take life for granted. I work among so many people and as I watch them day after day, I see that we are all essentially the same. Race, creed, colour do not matter. We are all the same people. Problems, laughter, joys and sorrows—we all experience them. My question today is why do we cheat? What makes us forget what we saw in someone that forces us into the arms of another? What causes us to not care about the feelings of another? I wonder if we ever see the other side of that coin. I know I saw it first-hand. However, being in a position to hear about others doing it and what their reasons are…fascinating. The most recent excuse I heard is, "It's so much fun." The act of the doing is so much fun during the moment but the aftereffects, the fighting, the lack of trust and the arguments are no longer fun, are they? Why not leave and enjoy your fun without the aftermath? Is it really that hard to walk away if it means getting what you ultimately want in the end? Or is it easier to stay and fight for something that you threw to the side so willy-nilly? I have a lot of questions and often do not really find the answers I seek. However, without the questions, there will be no answers.

Men will say they cheat because their women became boring and women will say they cheat because their men did not appreciate them. The same answer from above rings true in my head. Walk away. Start fresh and find what it is that you really want. The sad thing is that 'once a cheater, always a cheater' as there will always be a reason to cheat rather than to simply move on.

I find it so interesting when someone will say that they are ready for a relationship and yet when one happens, they only want to have their space. The irony is in the unfolding indeed—to listen to the story of the constant texting and phone calls and always wanting to spend time. Well, one would think that is what a relationship really is…making time for your partner. However, when your partner wants everything but you, perhaps it is time to move on.

We all dream of a better tomorrow—filled with love, joy, abundance, happiness, peace and safety. As I learn daily, all these wishes are within our control to create for ourselves. Yet, we seek it in others; why? My questioning mind wonders. Where or when is the next best thing? I have found joy in my solitude and yet I see so many others who find anguish in the same solitude. My question then is do I alone have the answers or do we each hold them in our own hearts and minds? Each person's idea of happiness lies within us all. The key to finding it is by doing what we truly enjoy. How do we find this joy? How do we know what we would like to do? This comes from doing something that is work but does not feel like work at all. In the end, we have to take each moment that we have on this earth in our stride in the hope of a greater tomorrow. There is a meme that says, "I want to slide into the grave sideways with a body that has been well used." Is this really true? Is the life we have worth living to the fullest? I think it may very well be. I want to be as happy as I can in this world. I want to have the love of my life, have a family of my own and see life through renewed eyes.

I met a man yesterday. Well, by met I mean online. I do not even know his name, just a handle. We chatted loosely over the few hours that we call days. One of the questions I asked was what he was doing with his Saturday night. There was no response until today when he said that he was spending time with one of his FWBs. Now, my first instinct was to be upset but then I realised he was being honest. We say we want honesty; yet when it comes, we are immediately defensive. I, in turn, ignored the comment and continued with the conversation. Ignoring it was to say it was all good. *Was it really?* I immediately wondered if that was what he wanted from me. Yet I did not ask if that was what he was looking for. Come to think of it, I never asked in any way what he was looking for. Instead, I continued to chat, not really saying anything of any substance. Then again, another man had messaged me, and in a moment had provided a phone number. Did I use it? No; in fact, I acted as if I had not seen it. When I do choose to use it later on, I have already planned my excuse. What is the point of all these pointless games? How do we plan to get anywhere in life? How do we meet people anymore? Nowadays, meeting someone without the use of the internet is considered organic. A term we normally reserve for produce grown without the use of chemicals is now used for people meeting people without a keyboard. Wow!

As I sip my white wine and contemplate that very word 'organic', I think back to my 20s when the world seemed so simple. We met people, men all the time. So much so, that it was taken for granted. In my 30s, it was still relatively simple to meet men. I mean, the one I met and married was not ideal but we live and learn. Now in my 40s, I long for even a fraction of those moments (the good ones). Alas, the time has passed and in 20 years, the world has almost become unrecognisable. Even sex is not the same. There are names for things that no one even thought of years ago. You can find sex online behind every keystroke these days. From fat to ugly to needy to desperate…everyone is selling themselves for a price. Are we, as the human race, not worth more than this?

More wine…let me tell you a story. The story of a kiss…the one that every girl dreams of from the first moment she discovers boys. That perfect soft kiss. The one that means he loves you or wants you or wants no one else. That is so much for a kiss. One kiss. Is it possible that one kiss could hold so much power? Yet, as women, little girls, we dream of this mythical unicorn kiss. What will it feel like? His soft lips pressed gently yet firmly against mine. Our mouths slightly open. Caressing each other softly. His hand raised to my cheek (as we often see in the movies)— not really sure why the hand on the face is necessary but alas, it is what we see on television so we hope for it as well. Sadly, my experience with the kiss has fallen short of all of the above. My best kiss came from a girl. No, I'm not gay; however, like Katy Perry said, "I kissed a girl and I liked it." It was not so much that it was a girl; it was the kiss. It was what you hope to get from a guy but sadly, men and kissing is like a snake that does not hiss. It is not their strong point. Unless of course, they are trained by a lady who knows how she wants to be kissed. I have had to train a frog or two myself and yet, no spark. In yet another pop culture movie, we learn that this so-called spark was invented by men to lure women into believing that if it is not there, he is not the one. But how do we really know who is 'the one'?

What are the signs of this so-called 'one'? Hmm…We daydream about movie stars and musicians and wonder where in the world all these hot men are. Because if you are like me, all the older-than-dirt men seek me out. What the heck; if I look like I am young enough to be your daughter, keep it moving. But no, the older men seem to think they have a chance and it gets really depressing for me. That is why I am now content being single. I want the hot, sexy, movie star-looking man to sweep me off my feet. Well, what the hell, which woman does not? They say you do not pick who you fall in love with and that men go after what they want, no matter what. Is all this really true?

How do we know what our future holds or what our true destiny really is? I often wonder. Let me tell you my story of how I got here—'here' meaning content being single!

Help! Somebody Help Me!

My cries fell on deaf ears. The shock that this could really be the end flashed before me. It was genuinely my last thought. I feared for my life. For the first time ever, I was petrified! What did I do to deserve this? How did I get here? How can I get out of this? HELP! The word came out louder and more pronounced. I was scared. I was horrified as to what was happening. What was I thinking? Why couldn't I have kept quiet? Why couldn't I have kept my mouth shut? Oh my God! HELP!

None of these thoughts entered my mind during the actual beating. There was a void of nothingness. I was in the fight for my life. I had to survive. My will to live was much stronger than any fear. That is how you know your true worth, when you stand in front of someone that you love more than life itself and yet you will not give up. That is the truest test of strength. I had to win, especially when winning meant my life.

My shirt was torn, half falling off my shoulders. My braids flying everywhere, some of my own hair on the ground ripped out during the tussle. No shoes, no glasses and out the door I ran as he searched for a knife in my very own kitchen. I ran. That is all I could do. No keys. Nowhere to go and did I mention it was November in Canada!

This was the fight that changed everything. It changed how I viewed my life. It changed how I interacted with others, especially men. It changed me. When you are faced with near death, it does something to you. It changes your very core.

I remember being in my 20s and watching Eve's video— Love is blind! I told myself that I could never be that girl. I would never be a battered wife, girlfriend or lover. I would fight back. I would walk away. All of that was brave talk for someone who had only seen respect from the opposite sex, who was independent and free! Who knew what she was about and had never truly been in love, or the toxic version that put me in the lowest place of my life in mid-November 2011. I stood outside in the cold winter air, barefoot and bewildered. I made an attempt to go back inside through the balcony window, the very window or patio door that he came in from. It was now dark outside; it couldn't have been later than 6 or 7 o'clock…with winter, it is hard to tell as the sun sets so early. Anyway, he locked the door right as I reached it. No tears were falling yet. Then he appeared at the front of the building, after what felt like forever, carrying my keys. He handed them to me almost as if nothing had happened. With the same swift attitude change, he scolded me for making him mad and then told me to go inside.

The way the front of the building is set up, there are two doors. After a certain time of the night, the outside door locks and you need keys for both doors. I was between the two doors when he left. He had parked in the neighbour's stall. Instead of opening the door right away and going inside, I watched him back up. In a moment of anger and bravery, I gave him the finger and yelled God only knows what. Before I could even open the second door, he was on me. In a chokehold, he dragged me back to my apartment straight to the kitchen where he found the biggest knife that I had and put it to my throat. I won't lie, I peed. Yes! I peed a little. I can say a little now, but honestly, I don't know how much. I know I wet my pants. He was screaming at me. I was sore, hurt, battered and bruised and I could hear myself apologising to this man. This man who had beat me to a pulp and now held a butcher knife to my throat. Who does that? I found myself reasoning with this man through my tears and sobs and pleas for my life. It was OK. Was it really?

There are many things I will share in this epic tale of survival. I want each person to take something away from my journey to self-discovery, finding the real me again. I want each person to find an affirmation that will get them through each and every day. Mine is this:

I am a winner!
I always win!
I win at love!
I win at life!
I win the lottery!
I win at removing this emotional weight!
I am a winner!

They are simple words. They came to me last week after a morbidly upsetting call with the man who I allowed to put me in a perpetual state of fear, seven long years ago. Yes, time flies and wounds heal. The scar on your heart can remain forever if you let it. The key is to allow yourself to heal, to move on and most importantly, to NOT identify with the term 'victim'. I was victimised; however, I am no victim. I am a survivor! Learn to love again, unconditional love. The person who deserves you will find you. Stop looking and the right person will become a part of your world. You can be you, through and through. No pretence, no faking and no wishing that you were someone else. It is being in the moment and being the most real that you can be.

It has taken me a long time and today, I am ready to tell my story without anger or animosity. In fact, I am grateful for the experience. It is not something that I would wish on my worst enemy; although, I am free of enemies. (Well, that I know of.) However, without the experience, the opportunity that I have to share with you would have been lost. This healing, this knowing, this unique understanding would be a fact for someone else to share. However, it is my civic duty to help someone to grow and heal and learn from my experience. My life's purpose is to help. So here we go.

No one came to my aid that fateful night when I called out for help. I am here to guide you through how you, as a person, can begin to survive the abuse addiction. I have! Now it is your turn. Walk with me.

How Did I Get Here?

Headstrong and full of energy, I worked away from home. In a lonely camp. So many people; however, it may as well have been only me there. I was dating a guy in another country. He was great—kind and understanding! One night, he asked me a peculiar question: "What would you do if you were pregnant for me and you found out that I had another girl pregnant too?"

This question rocked my world. Here I thought we were doing well. Making plans to build a house, a life, together. I was only 33 at this time. We had been dating for over a year. I, being the headstrong young woman that I was, decided that I did not like the question. We debated the question. He explained that this had happened to a friend of his and so he thought that he would place the question to me. The problem was that this information did not come out until after I was clearly upset. There were other factors that ultimately played a role and without warning, I ended the relationship. The key to successful long-distance relationships is trust! Open communication. We were young and so it was over.

A few months later, I met a man. He was a friend of an estranged cousin. It was the day I had purchased the vehicle that I drive today. He saw me, thought I had money and wanted a piece of the action. He portrayed himself as someone who was somewhat flamboyant, kind and arrogant. He made me laugh, which is very important to me.

Recently, I saw a video with Madea (Tyler Perry). She said, "Some people are only meant to be in your life for a season and some for a lifetime. The problem is we try to make the seasonal people stay for a lifetime!" Powerful words and sums up my ex-marriage in a nutshell. He was supposed to be a rebound! I married my rebound. I am racing ahead.

The day I bought my vehicle, my cousin decided to pick up Jason aka Crosses Crisis (to protect the guilty, I will not use real names). We spent the day together as my cousin was job-hunting and agreed to drop me off at the dealership. Jason told my cousin that he knew of some places that were hiring. So all over the city we went. At each stop, Jason would make more and more advances—simple conversation, nothing too pivotal. But when you spend a day with someone, you start to think that they are decent. He finally asked me for my number when we got to the dealership and I was signing the paperwork.

He said, "Write it down."

"I don't write my number down," I said. "If you want it bad enough, you will remember it!" Here I was thinking I was so hard. It was what is called a 'standard' today. However, back then, I felt pretty good about myself. He seemed nice enough. He fed me some lines about him and his girlfriend being broken up.

Let me pause here and interject that this should have been my first bright red flag! However, I was lonely, fresh out of a relationship, in a new city, dealing with an impending knee surgery, WCB involved, and the whole nine yards. I am not making excuses by any means; simply painting a picture of my mental state which plays a major role in my tale.

I knew all this about him, which was really nothing. He had a job, was in the tail end of a 'bad relationship' and he somehow seemed interested in me. He started texting me on a regular basis. It really did not take long. I felt uneasy. Texting was fine. I never wanted to spend time, not even alone time, with him. Red flag number two! My gut was talking to me and yet I ignored it. He did the sweet talk for a few months.

So, to establish a timeline: we met on 5 February 2009. I had knee surgery on 3 March 2009. We got married on 19

September 2009, exactly five months and 13 days after our initial meeting. I knew in November 2009 that I had made a huge mistake as, after two short months, our marriage was already on the rocks.

I digress. My mom was visiting to help me during recovery from my surgery. She met him. Before their first encounter, I told her that Jason was a friend of Mike (my cousin, whom she was fond of) and he always wanted to hang out and I would say no. She met him and was not overly impressed. I used to call him 'Crosses Crisis'. He seemed so unlucky. This guy had more bad luck than a dozen black cats crossing your path on Friday the 13th during a full moon. Need I say it? Well, here goes. Red flag number three! I am racking up the flags, right?

After my mom returned home, I continued to avoid Jason whenever possible. We still texted. I had to undergo physiotherapy to walk again. Jason would occasionally come and give me a ride and even go as far as waiting for me to finish. He realised that the only way to get to me was to offer something that I did not have—companionship. The point is that I could drive myself and make my own way. He wanted an excuse to spend time with me and, silly me, I let him!

Being alone and being lonely are two completely different things. It would take me years to finally learn this. Now that I know the difference, this story—as it unfolds in my head, capturing intimate things on paper to share in the hope that someone will gain some sort of introspection from my errors—makes so much sense to me. You know what they say—hindsight is 20/20. Truth!

I thought we became pretty good friends. Well, as fast friends go, so to speak. One night, a buddy of mine was in town on business. I was so excited. I had not seen him since I moved provinces. So it was nice to catch up. Matthew wanted to go for dinner. As I lived downtown, we went to the revolving restaurant, La Ronde. Great food! I told Jason that I was going for dinner with an old friend, being the honest person that I am and considering that I thought we were becoming friends. Knowing that he had a girlfriend, I never allowed any lines to be crossed between us. I grew up with guys. I was used to having guy friends that I had never slept with or challenged our friendship on any level. Hence, Matthew looking me up when he was in town to go for dinner was completely normal.

Crosses Crisis called about four times during the dinner, although he knew full well that I was out. I answered once. After that, I simply let the phone ring. After all, I did not owe him anything. He had his life and I had mine. And that was red flag number four! Where was my mind during all these flags on the play? Yes, clearly ignoring each and every one. I even told Matthew that I called this guy Crosses Crisis and we had a laugh. Then he asked in all seriousness if this was someone I should have in my life. Great question, right? Too bad I did not take it at more than face value. I thought, *'I know what I am doing. I am a grown woman. I can handle a little boy'*. Yes, wrong again!

That dinner would serve to haunt me in my near future with my ex. In an attempt to justify his often-horrid behaviour, he would throw Matthew in my face. I never understood why. See, when someone feels immense guilt for their actions, they tend to project that guilt onto the person closest to them. In this case, my ex simply could not be friends with the opposite sex. He had to dominate and rule. As a result, my relationship with Matthew was confusing to him; so every chance he got, he would say random things like, "Why don't you call Matthew? He will have the right thing to say!" or "Why don't you go be with Matthew? I know that is what you want!" No matter how many times I assured him that this was not the case, it made no difference.

It took many moons for me to fully understand the transference of guilt that I was living in. When someone creates a scenario in their head about you and holds on for life, it is not something for you to change. The truth is that it is out of your hands completely. You should walk away from that situation, as I would learn from my brush with death. This misconception that we women have that we can change a man is exactly that—a misconception! No one changes unless they themselves want to change.

I am love
I am free
I do good things for me
I am happy
I am joy
Today is a new chance to smile
I love me

What Was I Thinking?
Clearly, I Was Not!

One fateful night, the tables turned. He called me with the sob story of a lifetime. His relationship was over, an epic fight to end all fights which even got physical. Yes, massive red flag number five! All this in the space of two months. I felt like I was consoling him, giving him my time, listening to him as he went on and on, talking about how he was not happy and something had to change. Sympathetic ears! Rather than being empathic, I started to feel that there must be something I could do. After all, I too was lonely and could use some company. I bridged the gap between friend and lover. It all happened so fast. One minute we were on the phone for hours and the next, he was asking to come over. Well, the rest, as they say, is history. From that night to me giving up my apartment, renting a house way out of our budget as I was on disability, to the afternoon we got engaged and the wedding day are a complete blur. I often ask myself, *'What was I thinking? Clearly, I was not!'*

Who does that—take a moment of sadness and turn it into an opportunity for sex? Yes, my ex-husband did. Sadly, not only with me but with many others while we were married. By November, as I mentioned earlier, only two short months into this farce and my gut started talking to me again. Something was wrong. It felt out of place. He was not as attentive or loving as he appeared to be in the beginning. He was very lax, short even, always sleeping and tired and, most importantly, always gone. He worked out of town, like I used to. I gave up my position after they had called me back to work once my recovery time from my surgery was up. My explanation was, "When would we see each other?" I paid dearly for that too. That is, however, a story for another day.

He started spending lots of time on the computer, never wanting to go to work. When he did go to work, he would call after a few days and tell me how much he missed me and wanted to come home. There I was, ready to please. Telling him, "Sure, it's OK; we will figure something out." The problem is that when you do this too much, it catches up with you. We fell into debt fast. I spent over $20,000 in a matter of months. I had worked so hard to save up as I wanted to buy a house. But as I mentioned before, he saw I had money and he did not stop until I had spent it all.

Now, no money, no romance and no trust left. He was acting funny. It would be later that I would discover the cheating. Oh my goodness, the cheating. This man was getting more ass than a toilet seat in a public restroom at West Edmonton Mall!

There was an amber alert flag that came about right when we were going to get married. I had this gut feeling that I should not be doing this. After all, I never wanted to get married and his proposal had come over the phone, nothing special about it at all: "We should do it; we should just get married!" It was more of a matter-of-fact statement than a proposal. When I was chatting with my mom as I do nearly daily, I mentioned it to her. She asked if I was happy and if this was what I wanted. I was not honest with her or with myself. Thinking back now, I knew that I did not really know this man. I did not feel right about committing myself to a life sentence with him. I told myself many years ago that if I were to ever get married, it would be once! I was not about to do this multiple times. Knowing this, I really was not true to myself. I thought, *'Well, no one has asked me to this date and he makes me laugh, so why not!'* Yes, there is the red flag! My own gut was literally screaming at me and still I bit the bullet and did it anyway. So much for cold feet. All I did was put on some itchy wool socks that I am allergic to and grinned through it.

Let me tell you this—these are not valid reasons to ever get married. They may be reasons to date or pursue a friendship, but certainly not marriage!

So here I am in November; he returns home from work. We spoke daily on the phone. He practically begged me to let him come home, he missed me so much. First night through the door and he was gone. Suddenly he had to meet a friend and did not want me to go with him. So much for missing me, right? November is the 11th month and the number 11 means changes. Change will come whether you are prepared for it or not. It seemed each time during this horrid experience, my gut started talking to me in November. And when my gut did not talk, God himself intervened. I thank Him daily for delivering me from this hot mess that I found myself in.

Although the signs were there that he was up to something, I had no proof. Suggesting it to him brought on fights. By suggesting I mean talking about anything that made me unhappy. Most words were used to simply shut me up.

The debt became too much and the house was driving us to a point beyond broke. We found, rather I should say I found, us an apartment that was more reasonable. This was where the first hands landed on me, yet I stayed. Like a fool! (One should not tolerate insults, not even from oneself!) I remind myself of this daily. Healing process! Trust me, it takes time. I digress.

While in this new place, I found a job at a warehouse. I had gotten very sick after the wedding. My body was displaying the signs of pregnancy. Although we were trying in theory, my monthly cycle did not change. However, I was nauseous daily. Nothing stayed in my body. I lost so much weight that I could fit in my high school clothes. Due to my illness, my job being really hard work and him not working, everything fell on my shoulders. I would pass out almost immediately after work. He was obsessed with his phone— always on it, texting, talking and googling—whatever; it never left his hands. This fateful night, I fell asleep as normal. I had the most bizarre dream.

I dreamt that he had gotten someone pregnant! The dream was so real. We were fighting about it. I was asking questions and such. Somewhere in the dream, it was like a voice said, wake up! It felt like a hand was on my chest, stopping my air. I sat up in my sleep with a huge gasp, propelling me awake. It was dark—5:36 am! Yes, I remember the time! There are things one will never forget. This was eight years ago, 2010. Anyway, I got out of bed and proceeded to the living room where I sat in the dark, reliving the dream. Then, as if a light was turned on, the whole room lit up. We were in a two-bedroom apartment. His phone was in the spare bedroom that we used as a studio. I thought to myself, *'Who is texting you so early in the morning?'* I got up and went to look.

"Ooh Pappi, yum…I wish I could taste it!" was the preview. I opened his phone; at this time, he had no passcode yet! It was from some girl. He had sent a picture of his penis. A married man had sent a picture of his penis to a stranger. No wonder I do not like receiving such pictures now. Well, that is normal. Penises are ugly and until you are faced with it in intimacy, no one wants to see that. Let's be real; they do not photograph well at all!

I was pissed! Who does that; your wife is sleeping and you are sending pictures of your dick? So I confronted him. Yes, I sure did. I woke him from his sleep and asked him about it. Lies, lies and more lies. Oh, it was a friend. He was sorry. He would not do it again. He was bored and I was sleeping. Blah, blah, blah!

After that, there was a passcode put on the phone. Yes, lots to hide. Oh well. Time passed. I was laid off from work. Here we were, back to November again. He came with a story that he needed to go see a friend across town. He left and came back with what seemed like some dead flowers. It was late so I made my way to bed. He followed shortly thereafter. He lay beside me and something did not smell right.

We started to fool around and I was on top of him and could smell a perfume that I did not wear in his chest hair. I asked him what that was. I was so mad. As I was sitting on top, weighing maybe 115 lbs, I started beating on his chest. "How could you do this to me? What is this? Where did you go? Did you sleep with someone? Why do you smell like another woman?" He grabbed my hands. This is like a blur. My hands were shaking; I had put this one out of my mind. But here goes.

He grabbed me, flipped me over and held me down on the bed. "Why are you yelling at me?" he said. "I did not do anything. Why don't you believe me?"

I said, "You are hurting me. So you mean I cannot ask you anything. Why do you smell like someone else?" I was being brave as I had no idea he would do what he did next. I kept trying to get free from his grip. The room was a good size and I had a queen-sized bed. We tussled around on the bed. Finally, I got free and jumped up. He was on me like a cat, telling me to take it back. That he did not do anything. He kept trying to put me in a chokehold. I moved as quickly as I could, dodging, ducking, but nowhere to go really. Finally, he got me in his grip and began to squeeze. I was scared. I have been trained in conflict management. I did security for years. I knew how to deal with irrational people. Thank the Lord for this training. It saved my life. I started to talk to him through gasps of air, telling him that I was sorry and that I understand that he was stressed. I know he would never hurt me (although he was trying to put me to sleep). I knew I could not allow him to knock me out. A sleeper hold is not easy to get out of. I had to keep talking—telling him how much I loved him and that I forgave him. At some point, I do not know when, he calmed down enough to loosen his grip. I slowly moved until I was free. I hugged him, reinforcing what I had said in order to be free.

That day, I died a little on the inside. And so it began! There are tears in my eyes even now as I tell you. My hands are shaking. It is like I am living it all over again. I am sorry; this is where this chapter has to end.

I will never hurt me
I will always be there for me
I have love
I have life
I am happy with my choices
I love me

Fear Took Hold...Why Couldn't I Leave?

It seems that every second after that fateful day, I lived in fear—never wanting to upset him—walking on eggshells, so to speak. I could not believe that such a thing had happened to me. I was the strong one. I was the one amongst my friends with the most mouth, the most attitude. I had gotten into fights with men before. For example, a friend that I was dating pissed me off so much that I punched a glass door. Not enough to put my hand through; I pulled back at the last second when I realised what I was actually doing. The glass on the door shattered in a spider-web pattern and the loose glass cut my knuckles. I still have the scars to this day as a reminder of the anger that I let a man lead me to. However, none of that mattered now. Now, I had become the one thing I never in a million years thought I would be. I had become a battered wife—full of fear, shame, embarrassment and, most importantly, guilt.

I am sure you are wondering why guilt. Well, I started to convince myself that this was my fault: if I had not pushed him, if only I had kept my mouth shut, if I had been a better wife. All sorts of ridiculous thoughts ran through my mind. I was extra nice. I had sex with him whenever he wanted; barely questioned where he went or what he was doing. One thing I did do for myself, one positive thing in all this. Although this may seem twisted, I spent copious amounts of hours on the computer researching, breaking his passwords, accessing his numerous accounts and finding proof of his cheating. I became obsessed. Remember that I was laid off, home on sick leave. I was losing weight at this point, scared out of my mind with nothing but time on my hands.

It is amazing the things you will do to keep your sanity in an asylum. That is truly what my house felt like. I made sure dinner was cooked. I kept up appearances for my friends who lived hundreds of miles away from me. The friends we made together or rather the people he introduced me to in his attempt at creating a whole new life had no idea. I began to get closer with the girls but was too ashamed to confess to them what was happening. I was trapped in the worst place on the planet—my mind!

In all, he put his hands on me five times in two and a half years before it was all said and done. He once tried to leave me. By this point, I was so broken that I begged him to stay, citing that I could not survive without him. I shed tears pleading with him to not abandon me. At this point in my life, I felt like everyone had abandoned me. I was suddenly back to my childhood days: my mom coming to this country, my dad dying, my stepfather telling me how he wished I was still a child at the age of 16, my sister moving out and most of my friends moving to the opposite side of the country. None of these things were really relevant to me before. When you feel alone, you find ways to justify these things, diving into a past that seems riddled with abandonment. I use the term abandonment loosely, as it is simply designed to make a solid point.

There was something sick and twisted in me that I could not explain. Not to myself or to anyone. I spoke with his mom. We had become relatively close and at one point, I broke down after the second attack and told her. Oddly enough, she did not have much to say. She did not encourage me to either leave or stay. (A dear friend enlightened me this past weekend by saying, "She tolerated you. At the end of the day, he is still her son and, right or wrong, she will always be on his side!" A powerful analogy at this late stage of the game—writing this book is opening my eyes for me.) She simply listened. I suppose that was really what I needed at that time, someone to simply listen.

I did everything I could to hold my tongue. I would try to smile through it and the word 'nothing' became my best friend. It was the proverbial answer to any question I was asked. I kept quiet. I love to laugh but you would rarely hear my voice. I got a job once I finally began to feel better. My mother paid for the medication during my sickness.

This new job was out of town. I would work 21/7, giving ample time for a cheater to do his work. I came home early one day as my spirit was telling me that something was wrong.

I had the very same feeling when I was home before. He was acting strangely. I would call as most of my shifts were at night. You know, the time that you expect your husband to be home waiting for your call or, at the very least, anxious to hear from you. He was distant, often in the car when I called. When I would get home from work, the house was pristine. I mean too clean. I know that he was a neat person. However, the house looked as though it was not even being used in my absence. One day, before leaving, I took pictures of our bedroom. I wanted to see if it looked exactly the same when I returned home.

This time I was determined to get to the bottom of things. There was something going on and I needed to know what it was. We had a fight—a pretty bad one, even throwing around words like "I was impossible and maybe we should end it." This relationship was beginning to affect my job. I spoke to my supervisor and explained that I needed to go home. However, I did not want to leave early. I simply needed to be home when he did not know I was coming. My supervisor allowed me to switch from nights to days in the same shift. So I would gradually go to work earlier and I would be on the day shift in a matter of days.

I walked into our home, yet another apartment that I had found for us when the rent became too overwhelming. Yes, we moved a lot. By this point, I had a few good friends. The scene that I walked in on that night was quite bleak. I got a ride home from a co-worker from the bus depot. All the lights in the apartment were on. I walked in through the back door of the complex so as not to make him aware that I was home early. When I opened our apartment door, there he was on the couch with another woman.

I had been supporting this man once again—working my ass off out of town and sleeping in a new bed every shift for eight long months of night shifts. And here was this fucker in my house with some bitch. Yes, I called her a bitch as she had no respect. None! I walked in and she had the nerve to ask, "Who are you?"

"I have a key, do you?" I said very dryly and matter-of-factly. "I am his wife!" I continued. "I should be the one asking who you are in my house at midnight!"

She continued with some cockamamie story about how she was a friend and had brought him coffee. At that time of the night? Because not only was I born at night, I also fell off the turnip truck as well! All this time, he said nothing. Not one word did this man utter. There was silence, other than the bitch's voice and mine. And this conniving, undereducated, Neanderthal tramp…see what I did there? Yes, I called her the 'C' word. She had the nerve to sit there like she deserved to be in my house. My house! This bitch acted like it was her place!

I am not holding back about how I really felt but in the same breath, back to the story at hand. I walked into our bedroom and there was nothing that showed that I lived there. If one did not know, you would think that he had a bachelor pad. Our wedding photos were gone. Every sign that a female lived there was gone. He had cleaned the house in preparation for more than just coffee. Fucker!

For once, I listened to my gut. Dammit! It was right. Then again, I knew that it was always right. I remained calm in my anger as I knew this was going to get messy. I walked around finding more things. I pointed them out while this stranger sat in my house next to my ex-husband. (That couch, by the way, I threw it out!) She eventually got up and left.

I was very worked up after she left but I knew better than to try to start a fight with him. I stayed clear of him. He started asking what was the matter. Did I have a problem? To each question, my response was no and so he pushed and pushed until the anger that was boiling in my bones burst out. I screamed at him, "How dare you bring another woman into this house, my house?" Might I mention that the entire time he was badgering me with questions before my outburst, he had the audacity to text this bitch while he was standing in front of me? They were having a proper conversation. And I lost it! Straight up lost it. Not that it served me any good in the end. We were both standing and he grabbed my hands and dragged me outside towards our car that was parked on the street. I knew better than to get into a car with him in this state. Where would he take me; how would I get away? Would I even come back? Oh hell no, I was not getting in any car. He squeezed my wrists together so hard; 2 am in the morning and not a soul on the street. A police car rolled by on the main street. We were right around the corner for the police station in the neighbourhood. Ironic, wasn't it? They went on their merry way, not seeing a desperate woman in the shadows. I could not even scream when I saw them. His hand was over my mouth so hard that I could barely breathe. At that time, we lived in a very quiet family neighbourhood. Not much ever happened there. He dragged me to the park across the street and finally released my hands after pleading with him. Come to think of it, I did that a lot—pleading. He eventually calmed down and we went back to the apartment and to bed. That fearful sleep is unlike any other: that insincere apology in your ear, that voice that made every hair on the back of your neck stand up, the fear of never knowing when he would turn bad or for what. That fear has you walking on eggshells even when he was not at home; making sure that the ringer was always loud on your phone so when he called, you heard it. The reprimand for not hearing it could be like a lit fuse. It is a terrible thing, living in fear.

I will never hurt me
I will never let me down
I will never deceive me
I am she
I am me
I am free

This Is Heavy...Really Heavy!

There are so many things that I remember as I travel through these moments in my 'herstory'. Moments that I am not proud of. Lately, I have been having a lot of positive conversations with some influential people in my life. The profound details that we travel through is earthshattering.

Ever looked at a baby when they are attempting to do something new? They never stop until they get it or figure out what works. When do we lose this passion? Some will say, life. However, the reality is that somewhere along the line from 11 months old to adulthood, we lose the ability to keep trying. However, trying is a negative word; the better phrase would be that we stopped making an effort. Sadly, when you are in an abusive relationship, it falls into the same category. You reach a stage where 'making an effort' is greater than staying alive. At no point in the abuse do we realise that there may not be a next time. He may actually go through with it this time and yet we stay. We cover the blemishes and bruises with make-up or long-sleeved shirts and pants in the summer and turtlenecks in the winter. To this day, I refuse to wear anything too close to my neck. I have nothing to hide anymore.

"Thank you. I appreciate you. I love you." These were some of the things I would say to Jason towards the end. I watched 'The Secret' movie, taking advice from it to turn my situation around. I knew our marriage was in trouble. I tried everything I could to salvage what remained. I called a pastor into our home in an attempt to open the lines of communication between us. In fact, this made it worse; it was as if I had granted him the golden trophy for bullshitting me.

That was the night I heard myself—me—begging this man, who was abusing me, to stay. "Don't leave me!" I yelled. The sound of my own voice is in my head even now, as I write this. I continued with this beauty of a line: "What am I going to do without you?" This was it. The very first sign of the addiction taking hold.

I could not control myself. I could not control my words, my voice, my tears. That day, I pleaded with this man. I begged him, chased him around the apartment, dropped to my knees. All this drama. Anyone who knows me and has been in my life for many years will tell you, "That girl right there—we don't know her…she looks like our friend but the person we know would not be doing this bullshit." After the disrespect, the lies, the other women and all my forgiveness, this man was walking out the door—essentially saving my life at that point. However, that addiction! It had me basically putting my neck in the guillotine and begging him to cut the cord.

What Is Addiction?

<u>Addiction</u> is a condition in which a person engages in use of a substance or in a behaviour for which the rewarding effects provide a compelling incentive to repeatedly pursue the behaviour despite detrimental consequences.

Little did I know that at that pivotal moment in my life, I had hit rock bottom! There are two distinct definitions to being addicted. The first being a physical dependency and the second being mental dependency. I like the second one better although both applied. The second definition means being enthusiastically devoted to a particular thing or activity. This holds true with my above performance. I know that now! Back then, that was my heartfelt need and desire and want for him and all that came with being with him. I had accepted my status in life—a battered wife.

Jordin Sparks and Chris Brown's song 'No Air' is a great song. I love it. One of my classic go-to songs for sure. The message is so strong, "Losing you is like living in a world with no air!"

That was my world in that very moment; that was all I could think of. I was fired from my part-time job, got laid off from my full-time job and to top it all off, my health was failing. All this was happening and all I could think was *'How was I going to survive without this man?'* He was not working. He was spending what I was bringing in and his employment insurance. I was scared; I did not want to be alone. At this point, you are so damaged that you don't think that anyone else would want you. What was going to happen when he leaves? You are forced to turn your life around. However, the leaving is also a form of control.

At that point, I was on my knees when he decided to stay. He had won, for now. There was nothing that man could not tell me to do that I would not do. I knew there could be an ass-kicking around the corner, but somehow, I did not care. The words he used after he put his hands on me for the first time rang through my ears as if they were something to celebrate: "I'm sorry. I don't know what happened. You made me so mad. I will never do that to you again." It poured out of my mind like a kitchen faucet wasting water.

Words. Nothing but empty words. The very night that he was trying to leave, he was pushing me around for bringing the pastor, a stranger, into our home. Ironic, wasn't it? At least the person I brought in was there when we were both present; unlike the woman who would later describe the inside of my apartment to me. She had been there during the day while I was at work, for afternoon tea or, more crudely put, a casual encounter. The story sounds more and more absurd the more I write. That is the thing though; the only cure for addiction after the withdrawal period is self-love. That is the key that opens the doors to change in your heart and life.

Being able to love yourself after something like that is a leap of faith. With a support system in place, anything is possible. I know this sounds simple. It is easy for me to say this now. This was, however, seven long years in the making.

I own my passions
I own my dreams
I own my past and where I have been
I own my future
What will I see?
I own my present
I own me!

The Aftermath of Survival

So many things change in our lives and we manage to make it through. We always define ourselves by the bad things that happen to us. Why is that? After inviting the pastor into our home, things took a turn for the worse. We co-existed; however, I got the feeling that he thought I betrayed him. So he was rather cold. At that point, I decided that going back to working out of town would be the best thing for me to do. I had been taken off sick leave a few months earlier and had been working in the city. He was not working and what we were making was not enough to survive on, never mind live. As a result, I had been the sole breadwinner in the house, with a shopaholic who was spending it as fast as I could earn it on other women. We needed the money and I needed to be away from him. I needed to not be in fear, even if it was only for 14 days. I called up my old boss, mentor and friend, Roy, God rest his soul.

I called up Roy and asked if he knew of anything coming up. He mentioned that he was managing a camp that needed some administrative staff. He told me that he would let me know. Within a week or two, I got the call to go back up north. The shift was for 21 days, not just 14. When you ask for something, dream big. You will always get more than you could possibly dream of. I knew I needed to be away from Jason; I simply did not know how to do it. I did not know whether I was strong enough to walk away.

That job turned out to be a blessing and a curse in a sense. The blessing was that I got away from him. The curse—well, he had way more time to do his deeds. (Remember the bitch I came home to?)

This job would ultimately spell the end of our marriage. During my time away to cope with all that was happening to me, I ate and ate and ate. I seemed to be on perpetual night shift for eight long months and when you are working in a camp, there are snacks all the time. My weakness was chocolate chip cookies. The chefs got to know how much I loved the cookies and brought me a bowl of them fresh out of the oven. I did not eat the whole batch; I shared. The point was that I ate my way into depression, weight gain, solitude, denial and obsession over a man who would ultimately leave me. I would look in the mirror and not even know who was staring back at me.

I recently saw a picture of myself before I left for the camp job and when people were shocked at the difference in me, I would jokingly say, "I ate her!" Then everyone would have a laugh. Deep down, however, I would be thinking—when will I be her again? When would all my clothes finally fit the way they did in the past? When would I remember what it was like not to rub holes in the thighs of your favourite jeans and have to throw them out? Now when I show that picture, I say, "This is my goal weight!" It took a great deal of work and tears and drinks to get to where I am today. Most importantly, laugher, love and support from extraordinary family and friends and an insatiable desire and determination to rise from the ashes like the phoenix that I know I am.

Another benefit of this job was allowing me the time to really think and attempt to figure out what to do with this so-called marriage. I started becoming very miserly. My ex would spend money on anything. My financial situation before him was spotless; immediately after him, a hot mess. With my perseverance, I have repaired the damage and surpassed even back then, I could not even imagine doing so. I texted him constantly and tried to talk to him often when I first got there. Then I realised that he was not really trying to make time to talk to me. The first few months, there was some kind of minimal effort. But I could tell when I would get home for my week off that something was changing between us. I still had my fears but I was a bit stronger, a little more independent.

Interesting how every song played at the right time will give you a different perspective on what you are currently looking at. I just heard the Everly Brothers' 'Time of my life', the last song at the end of 'Dirty Dancing'. The words are so true. I sit here looking back on my past and then I heard: "'Cause I had the time of my life and I owe it all to you!" The time I experienced may sound violent, harsh, sad and depressing and believe me, it was. However, without it, I would not be here telling my story. It was the time of my life. It was a plethora of lessons that will carry me through the rest of my life. I am at peace with it now; hence hearing the song and working on this great piece of art brought a smile to my face.

Time passes
Yet remains the same
I am fluid, like the tides
I will ride to a better future
Watch me as I rise
Suspended in a reality
That I create!

The First Thing I Did Was Laugh!

I lived with my dear friend and her family. She essentially took me in. Months after the epic battle, I gave up my apartment. I had to do it for my sanity. I started drinking a lot when he finally did leave. It took a little over a year from the pleading incident and the ass-kicking that started this book, 'Epic Battle'. The drinking was only when I was home. As I mentioned, I worked 21 days and had seven days off. During those seven days, I got very little rest. I spent countless nights staring out the window. This apartment was on the ground floor, facing the front of the building. So I could see the parking lot. Each and every car that drove in and out of that parking lot was checked by me to see if it was him. This is what they call the withdrawal stage. He was gone. I was surviving. But there was no air. I could not breathe on my own, or so it felt.

Those seven days off from work were the longest days. During the day, I sat in my place with the curtains drawn enough to let some light from the sun seep in, not enough to show the neighbours that I was home. All the knives were in a pillowcase buried in my closet and the door was partially blocked.

I had to hide the knives. Seeing them out kept me in a perpetual state of fear. Having them individually put to my throat on repeated occasions is a memory I am in the process of forgetting. It has affected me though. To this day, I don't have many knives in my kitchen and none of them are very big, for that matter.

I knew it was better that he was gone, yet I longed for him to come back. I sent countless text messages to his phone. When he did not respond, I would call. I knew he was with that woman. The one I found him with in my house that fateful night, the same one who brought him coffee at midnight. Anyway, that is who he ultimately left me for. Here I was begging but cussing. I was hurt. I was angry. I was extremely angry. My therapist was scared, very scared at one point during one of our sessions.

Yes, counselling is the key. You need to talk to someone after you have gone through an ordeal like this one.

I was ashamed, embarrassed and humiliated. The worst part is that I was mortified of being alone. I truly did not know what to do so I kept vigil day and night for seven days a month. Watching, hoping, waiting, wanting and having no idea why. Most times I did not talk to anyone. When I did, I never once let on what I was doing. I would rush the call—it was taking away from my surveillance. Then it would be time to go back to work. I left and went back to being forced to focus on something else. When you are as hurt as I was during that time, you make the attempt to keep up appearances. The humiliation of what you experienced haunts you. You begin to think that the less anyone knows about your life, the better. When, in fact, the opposite is what you need. You need a support system. You need to be surrounded by people who care for you and can empathise. At this point, there is no room for judgement; although that is what you are doing to yourself the more time you spend alone.

By March 2012, I began experiencing problems with lifting my right arm. Of course, I ignored it. Over the next two months, it got progressively worse. I could barely type and that was a key part of my job. I knew this was not a work-related thing; however, I could not pinpoint what caused it. When you experience extreme trauma, your brain, in an attempt to protect you, tends to block out key parts of the traumatic event, which is a defence mechanism. You know that there was a terrible thing that happened; however, putting excessive detailing to it could be rather difficult.

I had an event to attend in my hometown in June of that year, so I would work a 28-day shift and drive straight there. That plan had to be altered greatly. My arm was so incredibly sore that I could only do my normal tasks. I went home and saw my doctor; it had become more serious.

My apartment was gone, my stuff was in storage and I was written off work. In less than three years, I had some of the worst health concerns in my young lifetime. So I was essentially homeless. I called and asked a favour and a kind heart opened her home to me. The Lord knew I had spent more than enough time alone. What I needed was a support system. And He gave it to me in the form of the friends and sisters I still have today.

And we laughed. A lot! I quite liked how I felt when I laughed and I began laughing at everything. At every chance I got, I laughed. When I first set out to laugh at anything, I had to force myself to laugh. Hearing myself, it would make me want to actually laugh because I thought that me laughing right now is funny. And so, the cycle continued. Then my friends would hear me laugh and they would laugh. You know that belly laugh when you run out of air in a good way and you gasp? That kind of laugh is what my fake laugh would turn into. I did it so often that it became natural to laugh. It is something that I practice now. It is through my perpetually contagious laughter that I am able to sit here and recount this for you.

You have to be able to laugh at yourself, at your situation and at where you have been.

There was a meme I read and perhaps even posted on Instagram that says, "When you can discuss your past without you crying, you are healed." I believe I am healed. One of the key ways I got there was with laughter. From my laughter, I got to love. Here we discuss self-love again. I learned to love something new and fantastic about myself every day. The first one was, "I love my laugh!" Find something to love about yourself.

42

I've laughed
I've cried.
I even died a little on the inside
I've loved
I've learned
This is not the end of my world
I control me and my destiny

I Don't Like This Feeling!

There is nothing worse than the feeling of rejection. That doubt that we end up pointing inwardly at ourselves. Asking the questions of: What did I do wrong? Why did he not want me? What is wrong with me? All the self-esteem that you built up over time seems to dissipate into our shoes. What brings this on? That moment when we realise that someone does not really want to be with you. There is no explanation, no reason given, simply radio silence. Nothing. Nothingness can be so loud. There are screams that would appear silent compared to them. That ache in the pit of your stomach as you search endlessly inside yourself looking for an answer that will never come from you. That instant is self-destructive.

In all the things that my ex-husband did to me, the action of indifference was quite possibly the worse—to live and see it each day. There was really nothing I could do about it and yet I stayed. His cheating was so blatant after a while; I mean, he left me for some chick, the same one in the previous chapter. She would end up putting him in jail (briefly). How do I know? Well, while I was away at work, my phone rang—a collect call. I accepted the charges as I had no idea what was going on. Jason was in jail! He made two phone calls as I suppose he was in the remand centre. He called me and his mom, begging for bail money. Apparently, he was facing charges of assault and theft of over $25,000. There was an argument and he decided to leave. According to him, "She was blocking my way out the door, so I pushed past her to get out of the house. I got into my car and left. Next thing I am being pulled over for theft.

Stealing my own car!" At this point, I asked how was that even possible. The car was registered to me.

"I signed it over to her," he admitted.

"Oh, really! That is convenient!" I said. "So you want me to bail you out? Why don't you call her? She put you there!"

He reluctantly said, "She's gone out of town for the weekend to her parents. She told me I would have to wait till Monday."

I could not help but laugh, "So she got you arrested for taking your own car and then skipped town. She's good!"

I had co-signed for the car for him while things were going well in our marriage. He had forged my signature on the registration papers so that he could have her insure it for him. Well, that backfired! When he drove away, she called the police and told them that he had stolen her car. Now, the BMW was in both our names as husband and wife at the financial institution. However, that means nothing; when those plates get run, the only thing that comes up is who registered the car and by default, it is theirs. He sure picked the wrong chick to mess with. The moral of the story is to be careful what you wish for; you might just get it and then some.

She knew he was a cheater; after all, that is how she and I even met. When he first left me to live with her, one of the things he would consistently complain about is that he had no privacy. She went everywhere with him and if he did not invite her, she would follow him in her car to make sure that he was going where he said. There is a saying that goes, "How you get your man is how you will lose him!" She fully believed this; otherwise, she probably would not have gone to so much effort to keep tabs on him. It is amazing the things someone will disclose when they need your help and now, with no one else to call, I was the listening ear. I know what you are thinking: how could I talk to this man? How could I even give him the time of the day? The problem is that during all this, I was still very much in the height of the addiction. It really did not matter to me what this man was telling me; what I was happy with was the fact that he was talking to me. I mentioned several times before that I kept texting and calling, hoping he would talk to me but, nothing. Now here he was in jail and no one to talk to, except me. Yes, I was depressingly happy about this fact. I also had new respect for her as she did something that I was not brave enough to do and that was to simply call the police. It did not matter that she used a technicality to get him away from her; what mattered was that she placed the call in the first place.

In the movie 'Why did I get married?' by Tyler Perry, I heard of the 80/20 rule, which states (I am paraphrasing, of course.) that your wife is 80 and her replacement is 20. This was so true. You have your good, good wife at home and you go out and find someone else thinking that they will do for you what you did not appreciate in your mate. Then they will fall short of the mark.

We all desire to have someone in our lives and when we finally have that, we treat them like the kings and queens that they are. Now when you put your all into it and then get nothing in return, it really hurts. It smarts. I loved my ex so much that I forgot to save some of that love for myself. I was so wrapped up in his indifference, his cheating, his mental and physical abuse, that all I wanted when he left was for him to come back. It was like I did not know how to live without him. I did not know how to make sense of him not wanting me. In order for me to finally wake up from that awful nightmare, I knew I needed to get away from everything. I needed to go as far away as possible to regrow my self-dignity. Staying in the same city, town, country as him was too much. I would keep making a fool of myself by begging him to come back to me. I have said in previous chapters that I drank a lot and oh, did I ever! So, coupled with everything else that I have said, let's put the biggest one of them all in the mix—fear! As much as he ultimately saved my life by leaving me, he had taken it away in the two years or so that we were together.

One day, I ran into a lady I knew from my hometown; it was nice to see a familiar face. We chatted for some time over the course of several months. Shortly after my friends helped me move from the potential crime scene that was my (our) place, she agreed to do my hair. At this point, I was already flirting with the idea of taking a trip. My shoulder was in enormous pain and no doctor or test could tell me what was wrong with it. It would be years later that I would remember the epic fight that began this book, where I was thrown into the corner of a hall closet, my shoulder making connection with the corner of the wall. It all made sense one day. I suppose in traumatic events, your mind, in an attempt to protect you, will bury them.

I digress. I went to this lady's house, she did my hair, we had a nice meal and on the way home, I got a call from my ex. He was livid! Screaming at me relentlessly. To be perfectly honest, I really don't remember why or even remember the conversation in its entirety. The only thing that sticks out is when he asked, "Where are you coming from?" My heart sank to my feet. Could he see me? Was he in the same neighbourhood that I had just left? Now let me paint the scene: I was on the highway at night! My friend's house was out of town. There was no way that he would have ever seen me. The road was quiet. But fear is such a powerful thing. I was not doing anything wrong. I was minding my own business, living my life. He left me. He moved out and I came back to an empty apartment. He even took things that were mine. I lived in that sadness for another six months after he left, long enough for him to nearly kill me. Now many months later, I was still afraid. I was staying with my dear friend and her family. I felt safe there, once inside the walls. On the road, it was a different story.

Showing him clearly that I was flustered, I asked, "Why?" He proceeded to tell me that he saw what looked like my vehicle go by him. I quickly asked where he was and he said northside. I released a breath. That did not matter because the initial damage was done. As I hung up the phone and continued on my way to my temporary home, I decided then and there that I needed to leave. I needed to be as far away from that man as possible. Oh yes, the fight was about me texting incessantly. Remember I began the chapter with making a fool of myself? Well, in that dark, weak and vulnerable moment, I took every chance to do just that. So I knew in my heart of hearts that I needed to go somewhere, that this behaviour was not an option. I needed to leave the country. For my sanity, for my own wellbeing, for everything that was good in this world to bring me back and take me over the hump of withdrawal, I needed to leave. Yes, I said withdrawal. I have mentioned a number of times how this man behaved towards me and yet I could not breathe without him. How is that even possible! I was an addict! I was an addict that almost thrived off being hurt. I did not know how to be without someone hurting me in one way or another. Hearing the word 'sorry' was like a rush. It was a reason for me to keep taking the substance that nearly ended it all, even after he left. How, how, how!

I can now say with all honesty that I did not like that feeling. So when I finally started coming back to the dating world after all this, I learned very quickly to identify indifference and move on. In Jamaica, they say, "Once bitten, twice shy!" I am not closing myself off from love; I am using what I have learned and continuing to grow daily.

Lessons are meant to be learned
Advice meant to be given
Not often accepted
Fear can be defeated
The first step can be the hardest
Walk in knowledge
And the path will appear.

Let the Healing Begin

Today I woke up and realised that I was alone. I was married, yet I still managed to find myself alone! *How did this happen? Where did I go wrong? I thought this was supposed to last!* All these questions were delusions. I knew better. Even as I was walking down the aisle, I had doubts. My gut was screaming at me, "No, don't do this!" But did I listen? Clearly not! Like squeaky shoes, you complain about the noise as you are putting them on, but you wear them anyway. That was me. I had more than doubts. A whole lot was fact. I only found out how young he was days before the wedding, 12 years younger! Yet another giant red flag. At this point, I have stopped counting how many red flags I missed. I am simply pointing them out. How was I going to marry this child? What was I thinking?

Over the years, I have learned that love is selfish. At first, I was outraged at the notion. However, as it was explained better, I realised that I too was a victim of its faults. When we say that we love someone, do we mean that we love them in the truest sense or do we love them to improve our quality of life? Good question, right?

Let's begin to dig deeper into the realm of love. What do you think was my take on love at the time? Clearly, admitting to being a victim provides the answer. Since he had been in my life, things appeared to be better in the beginning. Well, in the sense that I was no longer lonely. I have mentioned before that I gave up my job for this man. I volunteered to stay at home from a job that was paying me very well. I know now, that job was not my path. This is my path, sitting here telling you this story. Every decision that I have made up to and including at this point has made me the happy, strong, independent and single (and proud to be single by choice) woman that I am today.

Finding out Jason's age meant as much to me as throwing away a Kleenex after I blew my nose as I loved him so deeply, so soulfully. As we approached the wedding day, my guts could have jumped out of my body waving every flag on the planet and I would have, and did, ignore them. All I could see was that I would no longer be alone. I would always have company. He would be my life partner. I have seen great examples of successful marriages in my family. Differences overcome and life continuing; the difference was that these examples came from the truest meaning of love.

When you love someone truly, you set them free. I was not willing to set him free. In fact, he made me feel so special in the beginning that all the flags melted away. I did not see his lies. I did not see how much of a womanizer he truly was. I used to find it amusing to watch him flirt with other women. So obsessed I was with not being like his ex, so passionate I was about proving myself different. I lost who I was entirely. Even changing my name changed me. I could no longer differentiate between the girl that I knew so well growing up from this new me with a new name. I found it really challenging to adapt at first. This is what I wanted though, right? How easily I was steered from myself, plunged into this new way of thinking and being. I barely recognised myself in the mirror anymore—the things that I tolerated, the injustice that I watched and most of all, the sheer disrespect for me.

All because I thought that I loved him so much. All because I believed that this was the man for me, even after a phone proposal and an ugly-ass engagement ring. I love diamonds, so much so that my everyday jewellery is diamonds. As long as I can remember, I wore diamonds. I started buying them for myself as soon as I could. Matthew bought me a beautiful set, which I ultimately—I am not proud to say—pawned at the not-so-subtle urgings of my ex-husband. So when I saw what this man picked out for me and paid way too much money for, I knew that he did not know me at all! When we first went to look at rings, the saleslady said that I did not look like someone who would like big rocks. Not being myself, I did not agree or disagree. I was busy looking at the price and thinking that this expense could wait. Nonetheless, he chose something. We came back later on that day and he asked me to wait in the car. He was going to get my ring. When he came back, there was still no effort at a proper proposal. He basically handed me the bag. I opened it as we were driving away and it was the world's smallest diamond set in a sea of metal (white gold) stripes, shooting out from the middle to make the sparkle that was my rock look bigger. The stones in my ears at the time were bigger.

My blind love lied. When that man asked me if I liked the ring, I said yes. All I was thinking was *'Dude, look at my ears and see what I bought for myself'*. I should have turned those very words inwards to myself. Like I said, signs after signs. However, this love that I had was so extreme and intense, I suppose that is what made everything that happened in the next two and a half years seem so extreme and intense. There was nothing else. We knew no other way to be. That, my friends, is not love. That is an excuse to use someone else to improve your way and quality of life.

We all know that you have to find inner peace before you can even begin to love or think that you love another. And if you do not know this, then I am here to tell you. I had to find peace with myself and the world in order to love myself, in order to love my life, in order to someday love another. We are all energy and love. We are all a part of something great, fantastic even, starting by loving yourself. At first, it is really, really hard. However, you have to keep reminding yourself that you love you. Repetition is the way out. Sadly, it was the way in too. I have said it before, being lonely and being alone are two completely different things. When I got married, I was lonely and in love with the idea of not being alone anymore. Now I am alone and far from lonely. Funny how that works. It takes patience, understanding and love for yourself to begin the healing process. The embarrassment, anger, shame and disgust for yourself will pass. As Prince EA says, "You are not depressed, depression is like a cloud that is passing and you are the sky." I am paraphrasing a bit; however, that is the gist that I got from the message.

I learned that we all identify with what we are feeling as not being our true selves. When, in fact, feelings change like the weather. So, like clouds, this too shall pass. The anger, embarrassment, guilt and, yes, the shame—you will slowly replace them with pride in yourself for how far you have come, for surviving and now living. With love for you and renewed appreciation for all that you see. With compassion for the women and men out there much like yourself. It is not easy to live with abuse and smile. It is an even harder path to move on with your life and live again and allow yourself to breathe. God gave us free will. The sooner we exercise our right to find peace in our hearts, the sooner we are all free.

I faced my fears
I hold my head high
No more shame
No more blame
I am proud of who I am
My wounds may not define me
My scars have healed
I am a powerful being
I am energy

Anyways!

I had a good opportunity and I did not take it.

It is funny how things happen in our lives and we wonder what would have happened if only we...I had a good opportunity and I did not take it. Isn't that the sentence? Oh, how I wish sometimes to be someone else. However, we all know that is nothing but a pipe dream. As a little girl, you dream of your prince charming. Then one day, you realise that you let him go. After kissing many frogs, you think if there is ever a chance for being better than I am now. It is a great question, and as we get older it becomes more challenging to meet people, whether of your own age or not. Your social circle drastically changes and now the thought of being in a bar full of millennials seems far less appealing.

I never thought that I would be back on the dating scene after being married. Although when I was younger, I did not believe in marriage. I thought that if I ever met the right person and walked down the aisle, it would be the first and only time I would do that. I would always say, "I am doing this only once." I told Jason this many times. It was so funny that he used that very line on me seven years later. I was furious! How all this started was with a phone and a phone call.

We had amassed a huge amount of debt (in my name) during our two and a half years together. It took me seven long years to pay it off. For the first bit, I was working but did not really know how much I owed. I got tired of the debt collectors' calls. Then one day, I started answering them. See, there was virtually nothing that I could get on my own without help. Yes, my credit was bad. I could not even get a phone. It was quite sad. The cell phone account that I had and used up until this very year was Jason's. Yes, he had gotten us phones back in 2011. I know I am good at paying my bills, and long after we broke up, I had very little choice but to keep the phone and the number. I was not allowed to even change the phone as I was not the lead contract holder. So for seven long years this man could call me at will.

Time would pass and I would not hear from him at all; then out of the blue, there he would turn up again like dust on furniture. No matter how hard or often you cleaned, it still came back. I mean, there are other analogies that I could use but why be gross! Anyway, the calls got to be too much. It is hard to heal when someone calls you randomly once the withdrawal period is over. The kicker is that he never called from the same number. Why did I answer? Over the course of the years, I began to save all the numbers that he called from. I assigned him a special ringtone which would say, "This is your ex calling, crisis ringtone. Please take a moment to remember why you no longer talk to your ex. You have labelled this person as an ex for a reason. X does not mark the spot; X is more like the sign for poison! Think of your ex like a tumour that you had recently removed. Would you ever think to yourself, 'Gosh, I sure miss that tumour; let's put it back in?' No, I don't think you would, so why would you answer your phone? To sum it all up, your ex like is a poisonous tumour." I found it in an app I had downloaded. Anyway, I only ever heard the ringtone once and that was a few months ago when I decided to write this book.

He called one day in February. He did not sound like himself at all…his voice was all messed up. He asked things like when did we officially separate and such. I questioned him as I did not recognise the voice—I asked for his birthday, his mom's name, sister and all that. I even went as far as to ask where we got married. He answered everything and said that he would call back. Shortly after this, I was talking to my mom and she suggested that I contact either his mom or sister to find out if he was OK, thinking that it could be an attempt at identity theft. In the back of my mind,

I knew he did not pay for anything so who would really want to steal his identity! I chuckle to myself even now.

I was on my way to the dentist when he called back. The first thing he tells me is that he has a child! Asshole. During our time together, we tried and tried for a baby. But nothing. I know now that God never intended for me to have this douchebag's kid. So I have not heard from him in over a year and here he is out of the blue, wanting information about when we broke up. He was doing his taxes! Then he goes on to tell me that he has been ill and he is not sure what is happening with his health. Then he tells me about his baby's mother and that "being with her is nothing compared to being with you." To this day, I have no idea how to take that. I asked, "What does that mean?" and got bullshit for a response.

I told myself to be nice as I had finally finished paying all the debt that was in my name and the only thing that I wanted was my phone to be in my own name. I had spent many years building up the credit on the phone and I was not about to let him have it. Petty, I know, but if the phone was signed over to me then the old line would become dead and nothing could be used or taken. So I continued with the infuriating chat, knowing full well that we were divorced; he had been in a rush for the first couple years of our separation for that because he wanted to get remarried. But that relationship, much like many others of his, fell apart.

I posed the question, "So did you get remarried?"

"No. I am only doing that once! She can take half my stuff anyway. We live together; we have a kid. Why bother getting married?" he responded rather dryly, I might add.

My response (I must say, I am proud of this one.) was, "Really! Once? That sounds like my line. She can have your stuff…funny, I did not get that. I got 100% of the debt." Needless to say, the conversation ended rather quickly after that.

"We were having a nice conversation; why do you have to go and say that?" he sounded annoyed. As if we could ever have a nice conversation. We are not friends!

"I am just saying, is all, Jason. Stating the facts. Anyway, can you call the phone company and let them know that you want to transfer this phone to me?" I had to slip that in before getting off the phone. Who knows when I would get the chance to say it again!

"Yes, sure, no problem. Didn't I already do that?" he responded.

"I was not able to get a phone on my own back then. Now that I have paid things off, my credit has improved and I would like to have the phone in my name." I was attempting to sound as positive as possible with very little condescension for having paid all 'our' debt on my own.

"Sure. Let me call you back. I will let you know when I contact them." From his lips to God's ears. He was in no hurry to help me and now I had upset him. He would be even less motivated.

Almost a month to that day, he called again from a different number, saying that he had called the phone company but had not told them to transfer the phone to me as he wanted to keep the account. So what he needed to do was set up a phone on the account before the transfer. This would keep the good credit that I had accrued and I would be able to get my phone under my own name. Win-win for everyone involved, right? This meant that the account would not be closed.

After all the years and all I had done, this dumbass wanted all the credit that I had accrued as well. I agreed. The stipulation being that he signed the account over to me, regardless of what happened. While he was on the phone, I immediately called the company on a three-way call. I was not about to let him off the phone so that he could change his mind. We talked to a wonderful representative. Let me say that he was great! We both explained what we needed. The representative asked Jason if he would be signing the phone over to me. Jason agreed, saying regardless of what happened with him getting a phone connected to the line, the account could be transferred. That was a huge win for me as the calls were recorded. We agreed on a call-back time for the next day. It was late and I was onsite and was not about to wait up for a call back, giving Jason enough time to get to the nearest mall with his ID and get a phone added to the line. As we were getting off the phone with the agent, Jason said that he would call me back. I really did not expect him to as his words meant diddly squat!

He called back! The pit of my stomach ached; yes, you guessed it—for the first time in nearly four years of having the ringtone, I actually heard it from an incoming call. Aaaaaaahhhhhhhhhhh! We talked about how he did not want to screw his current woman over as they owned a house together and keeping his credit in good standing was important…yes fucker, the credit that I built up for him!

The long and short of this is that he owed money on his line from years ago. The agent explained this to me when he called me the following day. The primary phone on the original account had outstanding charges and the company would not let him add a new phone without first paying the old debt. Karma! Bitch. Trying to still take advantage of me so many years later backfired. Now he could not set up a phone on my line to save the credit. He did not bother to answer the call from the agent the following day. Not surprised! This whole transfer no longer benefitted him so he disappeared. Sounds about right. The agent asked me whether I wanted to continue with the transfer. At first, I hesitated, thinking of the possible repercussions. What repercussions though, really? It was not my fault that he did not pay his phone bill. He had agreed yesterday that it could be switched even if he did not get the new phone. So I was really in the clear. This was the internal battle that I had during the moment of choice. I told the agent that I would try to contact him myself. The agent had tried twice—the first time, his phone rang out and went to voicemail and the second time went straight to voicemail. Clearly, he had turned off his phone. In my attempt to message him from my phone, I realised that he had blocked me. He could contact me but I could never contact him. I never knew this as I had never tried or wanted to contact him in the past four or five years before that day in March 2018. Hell, for our divorce, I had contacted his mom as I had no idea where to find him. With an uncontested divorce, he only needed to know about it and not sign anything.

I digress. I then used my work phone and sent him a text. Still so nice—telling him thanks for everything and to take care. I meant that from the bottom of my heart. I had fully forgiven him and this was the last nail in the coffin of what would be our past lives together; chapter closed. When all was said and done, I told the agent that the phone was mine and the old account was dead. "Can I change my number?" were the best words I have ever uttered!

Life will give you lemons
Life will give you roses
Life will give you opportunity
Lemons or roses
The choice is yours
What to do?

Many Have Loved and Lost!

We are creatures of habit. As human beings, we women and men repeat the same things hoping that somewhere along the line it will be different. The truth is that until we do something to change, the outcome will always be the same. Einstein's definition of insanity was 'doing the same thing over and over again, expecting different results'. We know better. We know that when we do something that makes us feel like crap, we should not repeat it. Children touch that hot stovetop only once. They do not want to repeat the horrible feeling they got the first time. Why is it that as adults, we seem to forget the pain and want to dive back into another bad relationship? You see the signs. It is not something new. The controlling behaviour remains even when the faces change. The disrespect remains even when the environment changes. We know the signs; yet we deny that they are what they are. Why?

My only answer at this juncture is that we are not happy with ourselves. It is called, in so many ways, self-deprecation. Self-degradation. We are punishing ourselves for something in our lives that has gone wrong many moons ago. We are in denial that we have a problem and like clockwork, we pick the very same people over and over again in an attempt to fix this void. The truth is that when you have not identified the source of the void, you cannot fix it. How will you know what needs to be fixed?

The same people that we pick make us feel great in the beginning and then slowly cut us down to what they consider to be the appropriate size. And here is the really messed up part—we let them. We allow these people to break through our defence which, let's be realistic, is not

59

very fortified in the first place. We let them tear down the walls that we build up, and not very strong walls as we don't want to be alone. It is the same as being an addict. One of the main reasons that people remain addicted to a substance or, in this case, a type of self-deprecating behaviour is because it takes our minds off our problems or some flaw that we have created as the issue. We drink to silence the noises in our heads. We take drugs to forget the pain. We are simply stifling them. They are still there and in fact get louder with every sobering moment. I speak of loving yourself. That is truly the key. However, it is hard to love yourself when you despise the sight of your own face in the mirror.

We face embarrassment after something we consider bad happens. We turn that towards ourselves and criticise our own choices. We beat ourselves up for making a mistake. Then we hold on to that mistake and allow it to be so destructive that even the world's most positive person would not be able to penetrate that exterior. However, we let some condescending asshole insult us because it is the way we are already feeling—you think he or she is sweet or the greatest thing since sliced bread. It becomes a vicious cycle. There are several ways to look at possible end results. Find a way to love what you see in the mirror. Find a way to forgive yourself for the mistakes that you made. Find an ounce of hope in the lies you begin to tell yourself until they become your very own truths.

Yes, I said it, 'lies!' You must fake it until you make it. Whatever you tell yourself, you are right. If you tell yourself that you are amazing, loving, caring and happy, you will begin to believe your own words. If you tell yourself that you are an asshole of epic proportions and a horrible human being, the same goes for that as well. You must start telling yourself positive things. You have already done the damage with all the negativity. Now you would not be reading my book if you were not ready for a change. I can only tell you how I was able to heal from everything that happened to me. As I mentioned before, the first thing that I did was laugh.

Then I followed that laughter with positive reinforcement. I told myself:

I am love,
I am light,
I am energy.
I love me and people love me.
I have a great sense of humour.
I deserve to be happy.

The more I told myself these things, the more I began to believe them. I began to believe that I was worthy of affection and not the kind that tries to kill me or lands me in a hospital or the morgue, but the kind that refreshes my very spirit. The kind that makes me excited about living and being the real me. The me that deserves greatness. The me that is empowered. I am free.

There are many possibilities in life that lead us to true rewards. You can begin by ridding yourself of any and everything that reminds you of the toxic person that poisoned your life and your mind. Remove pictures, knickknacks, anything that this person gave to you that will serve as a tool to engage your memory sources. Get rid of them. I told you I threw out my couch! This is the purge stage. In order to learn how to fully live without this person, you have to start fresh. You have to fill your home with things that you bought or that family and friends have given you with love. Fill your hours with love. Buy things that speak to your creativity. Find the part of you that you loved. Surround yourself with things from that era in your life that will remind you to love.

A key thing to remember is that your life can change by simply changing your perspective. Your mind is now your tool to shape and promote everything that you have ever wanted to do—for you, for others. It is like unshapen clay. It is time to do some moulding. The more you tell yourself positive things and begin to surround yourself with things of love and your desire, the more you will slowly begin to feel comfortable in your own skin again.

The next step is to find time to be alone. I mean truly alone. Maybe 10–15 minutes a day. As time goes by, you will be able to do it for longer periods. At first, you may feel that this is not for you. As with anything, practice makes perfect. We have to strive for greatness in order to achieve it. The point of this exercise is to begin to learn to appreciate your own company, to enjoy spending time on your own. My mom would tell me, "You were born alone!" and I later added, "You will die alone!" It may sound morbid to a degree. However, the point that I want to make is that even twins are born separately. We all come into this world on our own. What we do with the time in between is entirely up to us. We have to make the necessary changes to accept where we are in this world. Being alone is not so bad. We find things that we appreciate. Going to the art gallery or museum or reading a book. Sometimes taking a long drive in the countryside. Finding our inner peace to make us really appreciate the silence. Yes, all these things can be done with company; however, once you master the art of doing them by yourself and enjoying, then you can begin to appreciate what you are bringing to their existence rather than waiting for them to expand your horizons. We create our own destiny. We are who we are and we make the choices to let that happen.

We are a very judgmental race, especially when it comes to looking at ourselves in the mirror. We should remember that this is your world and everyone else is just visiting. When we look at a reflection of ourselves, the first thought is to seek for flaws. Why not look and see the amazing image that you have in your mind's eye? It takes time and practice. One day, you will get there. I know I did and so can you.

I am beauty,
I am free.
I am what I see inside me
Walk in my footsteps
Take a leap of faith
Come out on the other side of tragedy
With a smile on your face!
Life, like time, keeps moving on
Why waste it being sad?
Imagine a better day ahead
Live it, love it, be it
And in the end, laugh!
Laugh like you've never laughed before
Find the joy in being who you are!
Walk with me.

Conclusion: Finding Your Voice

One thing that I have learned from this entire experience is to speak my mind. You don't realise how much of your voice is lost in the transition of being you to being victimised. You forget that you have a voice and as such, cower to any and every person that offers you some resistance on your path to healing and self-discovery. The truth is that you need to find that voice. You need to find out who you are in order to stand up for what you believe in.

There are so many aspects of our lives where we forget to speak up. There are so many times when we don't ask key questions. Don't give standard responses at the appropriate moments. Don't do what we should in that moment and then spend copious amounts of hours regretting our choices. In so many ways when we don't speak up or do what we know to be right in that moment, we live in these regrets and it often brings us right back to that vulnerable state that you were working on recovering from.

I know I said that self-love is important. It is in fact greater than that. It is a must. Once you have attained the feeling of self-love, you will then have confidence in your worth which is also key to the healing process. You have to first love yourself. There are several stages in learning to love yourself:

1. Telling yourself that you are loved
2. Remembering how valuable you are to yourself
3. Believing the words that leave your lips about yourself

4. Seeing the things that mean something to you come to light
5. Being on top of your personal game
6. Remembering that life is way too short to take bullshit from anyone

Once you work your way through the checklists of life, you build the confidence in your worth and words. Once you believe in you, there is no one that will not believe in you as well. There are a lot of self-help books that will tell you to fake it until you make it. That is good advice and it can be somewhat challenging to believe in better days when it seems gloomy in your near future. However, the 'fake it until you make it' mantra is key. You start to believe the things that you are putting out there. You start to build up your confidence. You start to take stock in the things that you do on a daily basis. Things that will drive you closer to where you want to be. Before you know it, this is effortless.

At this very key point is when you find your voice, the voice that will continue to carry you through life and its experiences. That moment when you lost your voice was very tragic and scary and almost seems pointless now that time has passed; however, without it, you would not have learned how important it is to speak up. You would have taken something so precious and dismissed it. Letting people walk all over you is nothing that anyone wants, ever. No one wants to feel like shit or that their opinion does not matter. In all reality, it does; especially when it comes to your life and your existence.

We are a proud race of people. That is why bullying is frowned upon in our society. We take the necessary precautions to protect our kids from schoolyard bullies. However, we often forget to protect ourselves from the very same thing. Bullying does not simply go away as we get older. We learn two key things from bullies. One is to be afraid. Two is to stand up for ourselves. There is no in-between. As adults, we cower from our bosses, co-workers and colleagues. This does not make it right. Now I am not saying that you should march into your office and start telling people off or anything like that, although it might feel nice. However, if you want to keep your job, there are definitely more diplomatic ways to address these types of situations in the workplace.

Perhaps this is not the place for you to be working. Perhaps there is a greater purpose for your life. Perhaps you need to be inspiring people to follow their dreams, much like I am currently doing with you. One day, the light will come on in that dark room that is your mind and you will find joy in the you that you are today. When that happens, a voice so great, immense and powerful will emerge from within. This will propel you into a world that is free of bullying and self-deprecations. Stand up, rise to the occasion and be strong in who you are. We have to find all the things that we enjoy in life and enhance them.

With these enhancements, we can then be more confident in saying what we think and how we feel in an unbiased way; then the self-expression will shine through.

Today, I stood up for myself at work. It felt great. I did not allow a misunderstanding of my words to cloud what was actually said. I had to be proactive in my self-promotion. I am confident in what I do daily and how great I am at this job that I am in. This is not my be-all and end-all and as-such. I am reassured that there are greater days ahead of me, which do not include sitting at a desk answering phones for a company, which if I did not come in tomorrow would not miss me. At the end of the day, no matter where you work, you will be looked at as nothing. Well, unless you are the CEO or something. Everyone else below that may as well be dirt. So that is how I feel about working for the man, so to speak. We are worth more and if we do not set our worth down on paper and see it daily, we will miss out on the key things that our very full lives have to offer us.

The lessons that I have learned from nearly dying at the hands of another is to not back down, to learn and find my strength and to use my voice and my talents to make a better life for myself and the people I choose to keep in it. I am a great person and I will continue to grow in mind, body and spirit. I have a great deal of love, experience and life lessons to offer to anyone willing to listen or be taught. I am here as a beacon of hope and light. There is a way out, there is a way to survive and there most definitely is a way to live life again.

I could choose to live in a world of 'what if?' What if none of this happened to me? What if I had been more prepared for this crap that I just went through? What if I did not have a way out? What if I was too scared to leave? What if I did not make it? These are all powerful questions that I have asked myself. The answer is the same for each one. I had to experience this in order to fulfil my life's purpose of helping others. There is no one else that could have done and lived through this for me. I have been chosen for greater things. These are the words that have gotten me through each and every day leading up to this very moment—sharing the most intimate and darkest part of my life. If it helps even one person, I have done my job. God has guided me to you for a reason.

Abuse, whether it is physical or mental, is wrong and can rob you of precious moments in life. The sooner we identify whatever situation that does not allow for a peaceful sleep at night, the sooner we can be free of the bonds that restrain us from living.

There are several ways to identify abuse:

1. Does this make me feel bad more often than not? Yes.
2. Am I second-guessing myself? Yes.
3. What is wrong with what I am saying? Nothing.
4. Did I do something wrong? No.
5. Am I made to feel bad all the time for simple things? Yes.
6. Nothing I do is right? Yes.
7. Am I afraid to say what I feel or think for fear of a negative reaction? Yes.

If your answers match mine, then you are in a potentially abusive relationship or environment. It is time to seek help and find a way out. There is no shame is asking for help when you need it. We have to remember to use the support staff that we were born into or chose along the way. This support staff is our family and friends that we know and love, who in turn know and love us. So many times, we are embarrassed by the situation we are facing that we choose to hide behind closed doors, attempting to deal with things on our own. The trouble is when you have no more answers in your head. When the keeping quiet or staying out of the way does not work and the bruises become too much to hide, it really is time to speak up. Let's not forget the authorities. I know there is nothing where I mentioned that I called or ever contacted the police. It is a very key thing to do. I was in such fear that I never involved them. My mom and stepdad did. They filed a complaint on my behalf after my brutal beating. I also never told them of that incident and to this day, unless they read this book, the details have never left my lips in front of them. However, that aspect was done. There are many outlets that can be utilised. Companies have support systems where you can call in and get confidential support. There are also crisis hotlines and homes for escaping abusive situations. Please, at no time, feel like you are all alone in this struggle. There are way more people than you think that can help and who are also going through the same situation. Silence is not golden. Speak up and allow yourself to be free. It is time for you to survive the abuse addiction. I am ready and willing to help anyone who needs help. Walk with me!

Author's Note

I want to take this time to say, thank you! Thank you for taking the time to read my story. Thank you for taking the first step towards changing your life. Thank you for being open to change itself. Thank you for being you and wanting better for your future. I hope that this has been of help to you or to someone that you may know. God has brought me through this season and continues to guide me. Remember, all you have to do is ask for help and where there is a will, there is always a way. Good luck and God bless!